REPORT

RELATIVE TO

Establishing a State University,

MADE IN ACCORDANCE WITH A

CONCURRENT RESOLUTION

PASSED AT THE

FOURTEENTH SESSION OF THE LEGISLATURE.

O. M. CLAYES............STATE PRINTER.

COMMUNICATION.

To His Excellency,
F. F. Low,
Governor of California:

Sir: The Legislature of California, at its fourteenth session, adopted the following concurrent resolution:

"*Resolved*, by the Assembly, the Senate concurring, That Professor J. D. Whitney, State Geologist, John Swett, State Superintendent of Public Instruction, and J. F. Houghton, Surveyor-General, be and they are hereby constituted a Board of Commissioners, to report to the Legislature, on or before the second Monday of December, one thousand eight hundred and sixty-three, upon the feasibility of establishing a State University, embracing an Agricultural College, a 'School of Mines,' and a Museum—including the Geological collection of this State; and that said Board report such facts and considerations as they may deem important in connection therewith."

In obedience to this order of the Legislature, the Board of Commissioners beg leave to submit the following report to your Excellency, with the request that it be communicated to the Assembly, now in session:

We are, Sir, with high respect,

Your obedient servants,

J. D. WHITNEY,
J. F. HOUGHTON,
JOHN SWETT.

REPORT.

In order to a full understanding of the subject referred to us by the Legislature at its last session for investigation, it will be necessary for us first to set forth the action of the Congress of the United States, in making grants of land for the establishment and endowment of a "Seminary of Learning," and a "School of Agriculture and the Mechanic Arts." We shall then proceed to show what obligations the State of California has taken upon itself in reference to the first of these grants, and what it has, in general, bound itself to do for the encouragement of science and the arts, as well as for the cause of higher education.

We shall next call attention to the present condition of the funds derived from the sale of the lands granted by Congress for a University, or "Seminary of Learning," showing what course has been pursued with regard to these funds by the State officers and by previous Legislatures, and what is required to be done in order that the obligations of the State to the United States may be fulfilled. The Congressional grant for a "School of Agriculture and the Mechanic Arts," will next be taken up, its object explained, and the legislation necessary to secure it stated.

These preliminary statements in regard to the Congressional grants of land for promoting the cause of higher education in the State will lead naturally to an inquiry as to how far the funds already derived or hereafter to be received from the sale of these lands, will go towards accomplishing the objects which they were designed to promote; what action a wise and liberal policy requires of the present Legislature in reference to the establishment of the State University; and what the general principles by which they should be guided in this action.

ACTION OF CONGRESS IN REGARD TO THE COLLEGE OF AGRICULTURE AND THE MECHANIC ARTS.

An Act of Congress, approved July second, eighteen hundred and sixty-two, makes the following provisions for the establishment of Colleges of Agriculture and the Mechanic Arts in such of the States as may choose to take action under it.

An amount of Public Land is granted to each State for the purposes of this Act equal to thirty thousand (30,000) acres for each Senator and Representative in Congress to which such State is entitled under the apportionment of eighteen hundred and sixty-two, to be selected from the Public Land within the State subject to sale at one dollar and twenty-five cents ($1 25) per acre, if there be sufficient, and if not, then the State is to receive land scrip for the requisite amount; said scrip to be sold by the State, and the proceeds to be applied to the uses prescribed in this Act, and no other. In no case shall any State locate its land scrip under this Act in any other State or Territory; but its assignees may locate it upon any unappropriated land of the United States subject to entry at one dollar and twenty-five cents ($1 25) or less per acre; *provided*, that not more than one million of acres shall be located in any one of the States; and no such location shall be made before one year from the passage of this Act.

All expenses incurred under this Act shall be paid by the respective States, and all moneys derived from the sale of said lands or land scrip shall be invested in suitable stocks yielding not less than five per cent upon their par value, to remain a perpetual Fund, the interest of which shall be inviolably appropriated to the endowment, support, and maintenance of at least one College, where the leading object shall be—without excluding other scientific and classical studies, and including military tactics—to teach such branches of learning as are related to agriculture and the mechanic arts, in such manner as the Legislatures of the States respectively prescribe, in order to promote the liberal and practical education of the industrial classes in the several pursuits and professions in life.

The following conditions are attached to this grant:

First—If any portion of the Fund shall, in any way, be diminished or lost, it shall be replaced by the State, so that the capital of this Fund shall remain forever undiminished, except that a sum not exceeding ten per cent of it may be expended for the purchase of lands for sites or experimental farms, and the annual interest shall be regularly applied to the purposes prescribed.

Second—No portion of said Fund, or the interest, shall be applied, directly or indirectly, under any pretence whatever, to the purchase, erection, preservation, or repairs of any building or buildings.

Third—Any State accepting the provisions of this Act shall provide, within five years at least, not less than one College, as aforesaid, or the grant to such State shall cease, and it shall pay over to the United States the amount received for any lands previously sold, and the title to purchases under the State shall be valid.

Fourth—An annual report shall be made regarding the progress of each College organized under this Act, one copy of which shall be sent to all the other Colleges, and one copy to the Secretary of the Interior.

Fifth—No State, while in a condition of insurrection against the United States, shall be entitled to the benefits of this Act.

Sixth—No State shall be entitled to the benefits of this Act unless it shall express its acceptance thereof, by its Legislature, within two years from the date of its approval by the President.

From the above it will be seen that the State of California will be entitled to one hundred and fifty thousand acres of land, there being two Senators and three Representatives from this State in Congress, under the apportionment of eighteen hundred and sixty-two, and that the first step to be taken in the matter is for the Legislature to pass a resolution expressing its acceptance of the grant, and this must be done by the Legislature of eighteen hundred and sixty-three and sixty-four, otherwise, the period of two years, during which acceptance is possible, will have expired before action can be taken.

Furthermore, it will be observed that it is not imperatively necessary that the Legislature of eighteen hundred and sixty-three and sixty-four should proceed to establish a College under the Act of Congress, as five years are allowed for this purpose, and the Legislature of eighteen hundred and sixty-five and sixty-six could act in time to prevent forfeiture of the grant.

Still, it will undoubtedly be conceded that it would be better that some action should be had or attempted to be had by the present Legislature, even if only of a prospective nature, to prevent undue haste in the incipient stages of an undertaking likely to require so much preparation, and in which a well matured plan will be of so much importance to the future of the institution.

CONGRESSIONAL GRANT FOR A SEMINARY OF LEARNING.

By section twelve of an Act, approved March third, eighteen hundred and fifty-three, Congress granted to California seventy-two sections, or forty-six thousand and eighty acres of land, for the use of a "Seminary of Learning."

There are no conditions attached to this grant beyond those implied in the words "Seminary of Learning," the intention and meaning of which will be fully considered further on in this report, when the use which has been made by the States of this grant will be stated.

But the State itself has inserted in its Constitution certain clauses which bear on the proper use of this grant, as we will now proceed to set forth.

CONSTITUTIONAL OBLIGATIONS.

The State of California has assumed in its Constitution the following obligations:

"The Legislature shall encourage by all suitable means the promotion of intellectual, scientific, moral, and agricultural improvement." (Constitution, Article IX, Sec. 2.)

"The Legislature shall take measures for the protection, improvement, or other disposition of such lands as have been or may hereafter be reserved or granted by the United States, or any person or persons, to this State for the use of a University; and the funds accruing from the rents or sale of such lands, or from any other source for the purpose aforesaid, shall be and remain a permanent Fund, the interest of which shall be applied to the support of said University, with such branches as the public convenience may demand, for the promotion of literature, the arts and sciences, as may be authorized by the terms of such grant, and it shall be the duty of the Legislature, as soon as may be, to provide effectual means for the improvement and permanent security of the funds of said University." (Article IX, Sec. 4.)

From the above it will be seen that the State has taken on itself the obligation of taking care of the proceeds of the lands granted by Congress for higher education, of investing them securely, and of putting them to a suitable use "for the promotion of Literature, the Arts and Sciences," "*as soon as may be.*" This was in eighteen hundred and forty-nine; and yet, up to the present time, no action having any definite result has been taken by the Legislature in regard to either the safe investment of the Seminary Fund, or to the use of any portion of it for the purpose for which it was donated by Congress.

The lands granted for the Seminary Fund have nearly all been sold, and a portion of the principal received, together with a certain amount of interest. The books in the office of the Surveyor-General show that payments to the amount of twenty-eight thousand four hundred and eighteen dollars and sixty-one cents ($28,418 61) have been made to the State Treasury on account of the Seminary Fund, for principal and interest, while the books of the State Controller show that there is only about four thousand dollars ($4,000) standing to the credit of the Seminary Fund in the State Treasury. This discrepancy is not owing to the fact that any appropriations have ever been made from the Seminary Fund, but to the circumstance that the County Treasurers have not distinguished, in their returns of sales, between School Lands and Seminary Lands, but have given receipts to purchasers of lands of the latter class on blanks prepared for School Lands, and doubtless have paid the funds into the State Treasury in the same manner.

It appears, therefore, that legislation is necessary for the purpose of segregating the Seminary Fund from the School Fund, with which it is now to a considerable extent confounded, as also for effecting a determination of the precise amount of principal and interest which has been received on account of the Seminary Fund. As no period is indicated by the law at which the amount due for the Seminary Lands shall be paid in full, it is suggested that some steps be taken in this direction by the present Legislature, the amount now due being about forty-five thousand dollars ($45,000.) If the whole amount be not called in at once, at least some period should be designated as the time when it will be. This must be done, or, what is still better, the Act of the Legislature, approved April twenty-third, eighteen hundred and fifty-eight, should be complied with, *as has never yet been done.* By this Act provision was made for the sale of the University Lands. It was directed that they be sold, in the same manner, on the same terms, and subject to the same conditions, as the unsold portions of the five hundred thousand acre grant for the Public Schools. It was provided, also, that the proceeds of the sales of the University or Seminary Lands should be paid into the School Land Fund; and that, from time to time, they should be invested in seven per cent bonds for the benefit of the School Fund.

So far, the law seems to have been partially, and, indeed, to a considerable extent, complied with. The lands have been sold, part of the principal and part of the interest received, and the larger part of both paid into the School Fund; but the essential condition of the Act—essential, at least, so far as the integrity of the University Fund is concerned—has never been carried into execution.

It was, namely, directed that the Board of Examiners should, at the expiration of one year from the passage of the Act—that is to say, on the twenty-third of April, eighteen hundred and fifty-nine—take and use fifty-seven thousand six hundred dollars, ($57,600,) of any money belonging to the School Fund, for the purpose of buying bonds; and when the said bonds had been so purchased, that they should be delivered to the State Treasurer, and kept by him as a special deposit, marked "Seminary Fund," to the credit of said Fund. All interest paid into the Treasury on said Seminary bonds was to be invested in State bonds in the same manner.

But neither on the twenty-third of April, eighteen hundred and fifty-nine, nor at any subsequent time, has the Board of Examiners purchased the bonds for the Seminary Fund, as by this law required, and the consequence is that the School Fund has had the benefit and use of the proceeds of the sale of the Seminary Lands, and now owes the amount which has been received to the Seminary Fund.

It is time that this condition of things should cease, as it is in direct contravention of the Constitution of the State, and of the requirements of a Legislative Act. It is believed that the Act of the Legislature of eighteen hundred and fifty-eight meets this difficulty in the best way, and that it should be carried out, as far, at least, as the principal of the University Fund is concerned. The fifty-seven thousand six hundred dollars, ($57,600,) of University Fund principal should be taken from the bonds already in possession of the School Fund, and set apart as a special Fund, marked "University Fund—Principal;" or else a portion of the money now in the School Fund should be used for the purchase of new bonds to that amount.

But there still remains to be considered the income due the University Fund; that is to say, the amount of interest which would have accrued on the fifty-seven thousand six hundred dollars, ($57,600,) had the law of eighteen hundred and fifty-eight been carried out. The School Fund has been receiving, not only the principal of the University Fund, as fast as it was paid in, but the interest on the lands sold, at the rate of ten per cent per annum. The Constitution of the State requires that the distinction between interest and principal shall be kept up in relation to the University Fund, as only the latter can be used for the purposes of a University.

As it would be difficult to say exactly how much interest would have accrued to the Seminary Fund had the law of eighteen hundred and fifty-eight been complied with, the best way of arriving at a satisfactory result would be to allow interest at seven per cent per annum from the time when the Board of Examiners was required to purchase the bonds, namely, April twenty-third, eighteen hundred and fifty-nine, on the fifty-seven thousand six hundred dollars, ($57,600,) which will be twenty thousand one hundred and sixty dollars, ($20,160,) and this amount should be taken from the money now in the School Fund, and set apart as a Special Fund, marked "Seminary Fund—Interest." This amount would then be available immediately for any purpose connected with the support of a University.

We have next to consider how far the proceeds of the Congressional grants of lands will go towards building up an institution for higher education in California, and what, under the circumstances, would appear to be the wisest course of action to be pursued by the Legislature in taking initiatory steps towards making these funds available for the objects they were intended to promote.

For this purpose it will be necessary first to give some idea of the system of instruction (so far as the same can be called a system) pursued in the different educational establishments of the United States of a grade above that of a Common School.

A complete and perfect system of education, or public instruction, implies the creation of institutions for primary, secondary, and higher education. The Common Schools, or Primary Schools, should exist in every town and district in sufficient numbers to give all the children of the State, of both sexes, the first elements of a sound education. This much should be compulsory on all citizens, and should be the first care of the Legislature.

No child should be allowed to grow up in habits of vagrancy; and no State can afford to allow any one, not idiotic, to be brought up without being taught the use of their mother tongue, both in reading and writing, and furnished with some general ideas of history and geography, as well as of morality and religion.

In very thinly settled regions, like large portions of California, and with a more or less roving population, there will always be great difficulty in extending educational facilities to all children; but the greater the difficulty, the more binding the obligation, and no Legislature will be true to its duty which neglects to do all in its power to foster and sustain the system of Common Schools.

Next to the Common Schools, for the support of which the United States Government has, in the newer States, made a partial provision by the donation of two sections of land in every township, or its equivalent, comes the Secondary School—or the Academy, or High School, as this class of institutions is usually called in the United States. The Academies are institutions where all those of either sex who have the means and the inclination to advance a step further in the acquisition of learning than is permitted by the Common School may do so. The Academies usually teach two distinct classes of students, one consisting of boys intending to enter College, the other of boys and girls who are desirous of obtaining what is commonly called a "good English education," which implies a considerable advance over the Common School.

To illustrate the degree of advancement attained by the "Academies" or High Schools in some of the Eastern States, reference may be made to those of New York, in regard to which statistics may be obtained, as they are all under the control of the "Regents of the University," and required to report, annually, all the particulars of their condition, in order that they may share in the funds distributed by the Legislature to the Academies.

There were in New York, in eighteen hundred and sixty-one, in active operation, two hundred and seventeen Academies, with twenty-two thousand five hundred and sixty-seven scholars, about equally divided between the two sexes, having two millions eight hundred and twenty-two thousand eight hundred and forty-nine dollars fixed capital, in lots, buildings, Libraries and philosophical apparatus, receiving three hundred and sixty thousand six hundred and sixty-four dollars from tuition fees, and paying four hundred and thirty-three thousand and fifty-nine dollars as salaries to Teachers, of whom one thousand and forty-two were employed. In most of these institutions the following studies were taught: Greek grammar and antiquities; Latin grammar and Roman antiquities; mythology, French, German, anatomy, physiology and hygiene, botany, chemistry, geology, history and rhetoric, arithmetic, bookkeeping, English grammar, geography, algebra, astronomy, geometry, physics, surveying, and trigonometry. In some thirty of the Academies the study of mathematics was carried up to and including the calculus, which is as far as is usually done in our Colleges.

In some of the Academies of New England, and especially in the High Schools, which are free Public Schools in the large cities, the facilities for instruction are more complete than in many of the Western Colleges. The current expenses of the Academies in New England are usually paid by the fees of tuition, but the buildings, grounds, apparatus, and Library are generally furnished by the liberality of private individuals, so that the cost of education is much reduced from what it would be were this not the case. A well endowed Academy, in some localities, may be little inferior in its educational facilities, to some Colleges; and the chief difference would perhaps be found to be in this fact: that in the College there was nominally, and nominally only, a four years' course of study, which all are supposed to follow.

No provision or grant of land has been made by the United States especially for secondary instruction; although, in most of the State Universities a "Preparatory School" is kept up, which is in part supported by the same means as the higher departments in these institutions. This preparatory School answers in most respects to the Academy or High School, one of its main objects being to fit the pupils for passing the necessary examination for entering the Collegiate Department.

It would be interesting, in this connection, to be able to furnish a statement of the number of pupils attending the High Schools or Academies, as compared with the number of scholars in the Primary Schools; but the data are too imperfect to allow of this being done to any extent. In New York, however, it would appear that there are about forty scholars in the Primary Schools for every one in the Acadamies; and, to compare College, Academy, and Primary Schools, for every one student in College there are seven at the Academy, and two hundred and twenty-two at the Primary School.

We pass now from the consideration of the Schools for secondary instruction, to the institutions for higher education, including the Colleges, Universities, Professional and Special Schools of Science and Art.

It is only in countries like France and Germany, where there is one brain and one system directing all the details of government, from the highest to the lowest, that there can be a perfect system of educational establishments. In France, for instance, everything is subordinate to the Minister of Public Instruction; not a School or College that does not belong to a system, and have all its arrangements made in conformity with that system.

In this country there is neither unity nor conformity; neither Government supervision, nor, except to a very limited extent, Government aid, in anything beyond the rank of a Primary School.

Our highest institutions have grown up by degrees, adapting themselves to the increasing wants of the community, and spreading as the wave of population has spread, until there are now over two hundred so called Colleges in the United States. The American College is a thing *sui generis*—it is not a University, like those of Germany, nor a Gymnasium, but something intermediate between the two, and partaking of some of the character of both.

The German Gymnasium is often compared to the American College. "But," to quote the words of Professor Lane, of Harvard University, "in the nature of many of the studies pursued, the age at which the pupils enter, and the management to which they are subjected, there is as great a difference between the Gymnasium and the College as between the municipal institutions of Boston and those of the free towns of Bremer and Lübeck. The pupils of the German Gymnasium enter at a tender age, remain some nine years, and are instructed from the rudiments onward, while the age at which they leave the Gymnasium is not much under that of our College graduates. But, up to that time, they are treated as school boys. They are drilled and instructed by Masters, and sit in school from thirty to thirty-two hours a week."

Perhaps the nearest approach to describing the Gymnasium would be to say that it was a combination of our Academy or High School course, with the first two years of a College course. But in comparing German and American institutions of learning, allowance must always be made for what some would call German slowness, and which others, perhaps with better reason, would denominate American haste. Certain it is that the gymnasiast is considered and treated as a boy, while the American College student, already in his freshman years, looks upon himself as a man, if not so regarded by others.

The last two years of the American College course have no inconsiderable analogy with the University course of Germany. During these years the student is taught to a considerable extent by lectures, as at the German Universities, and is allowed some freedom of choice as to what studies he will pursue. The student, during the junior and senior years in an American College, pursues to a considerable degree such studies as would be taken by a German University student in connection with his, as we call them, purely professional studies.

Almost all the American Colleges require, nominally at least, about the same amount of preparation for admission to the lowest class; but in reality, there is a great difference between different Colleges in the strictness with which the examinations are conducted. Indeed, at too many Colleges they are but little better than a farce.

What is supposed to be required at most of the Colleges as preparatory for admission to the freshman class, is English grammar, geography, Latin grammar, Latin prose composition, and the ability to translate at sight from some of the easier Latin authors, as Cicero, Sallust, and Virgil; Greek grammar, and some acqaintance with the easier Greek prose writers, usually Xenophon; mathematics, including arithmetic; algebra as far as quadratic equations, and sometimes part of Euclid.

The Collegiate undergraduate course extends, in all our Colleges, over a period of four years, during which instruction is imparted both by lectures and by recitations. The first two years are chiefly devoted to the Greek and Latin languages, and mathematics, with exercises in declamation, and the writing of English prose compositions. During the last year of the course the instruction is, to a considerable degree, given in the form of lectures—physics, chemistry, astronomy, geology, mental and moral philosophy, being the principal subjects thus taught. Latin composition, and the study of the more difficult Greek historians and poets, are also pursued during the last two years. Furthermore, the application of mathematics to practical pursuits—as navigation, surveying, and engineering—is a prominent part of the course of instruction during these years; and practice in writing and speaking the English language, by compositions and debate, is continued nearly to the end of the last year.

The propriety of devoting so much time to the study of the dead languages as is usually done in our colleges, has often been discussed, and while almost all learned men are of opinion that this branch of study is of the greatest value, as laying the foundation of a thorough knowledge of the mother-tongue, and of European languages in general, nearly all of which are descended from the Latin and Greek, and as affording an excellent discipline for the mind, and training in habits of study, yet it has been often argued, and not without a show of reason, that the study of the spoken languages of Europe, especially French and German, is really of more practical importance to the student, and that it may be equally valuable as a means of mental and intellectual training. Hence, in several Colleges, as in the "Free Academy" of New York City, which although called an "Academy," is in reality what is generally known as a College, students are allowed, at their option, or that of their parents and guardians, to select either a course of ancient or modern languages, which they may pursue through the whole four years. The languages, studied by those who take the modern course, are French, German, and Spanish. Another way of avoiding the necessity of devoting so much time to Greek and Latin as was formerly done, has been adopted in quite a number of Colleges. This is the creation of two divisions of students in each class, after the Freshman or Sophomore years. One of these divisions follows nearly the generally adopted routine of study in which the ancient languages are so prominent; this is called the classical course. The other, or scientific course, gives the time otherwise taken up by Latin and Greek, to the modern languages, especially French and German, and also in part to a further study of the practical application of science, especially of chemistry and physics.

In former days the College was considered almost exclusively as the place where young men were to be fitted to enter one of the "learned professions," so called; that is, to become either a "Lawyer," or a Doctor of Medicine, or a Theologian. Indeed, the older Colleges, especially in New England, were established more with the aim of preparing for the study of theology than for any other purpose.

As a natural consequence, the Colleges gradually added to themselves, in many instances, professional Schools, especially those of theology and medicine. In these Schools the collegiate buildings, libraries, and collections were used, to some extent at least, and usually a part of the instruction was given by Professors employed in the College proper—the whole being under the government of one body of Trustees. Thus, the College became a nucleus, as it were, of a system of educational instruction to the whole body, of which the name of "University" might with some propriety be applied, understanding, as we do by that term, a place where the entire range of science and letters is represented, and facilities afforded for instruction in the same.

The Eastern Colleges have gradually developed themselves, especially within the last twenty years, by increasing the amount of information required as preparatory to admission to the Freshman Class, and by making the examinations more thorough and frequent during the College course; so that thus the general standard of scholarship has been raised. Besides this, quite a number of Colleges have added a department of instruction in applied science, or a "Scientific School," as it is usually called, together with other adjuncts, such as observatories, collections of minerals, fossils, animals, plants, models of engineering works, and a variety of such aids to instruction in the various branches of science applied to the arts.

Thus, Harvard University, besides the College proper, or undergraduate course, has separate faculties, buildings, libraries, collections, etc., for Schools of law, medicine, theology, and science, besides the Observatory and the Zoological Museum, which are institutions expressly calculated for advancing science, and not for teaching it. Yale College has also the four departments of theology, law, medicine, and "philosophy and the arts," or *science* represented in the Professional Schools, and the "Sheffield Scientific School," attached to the College.

Schools of law, medicine, and theology also exist as entirely independent institutions all over the Eastern States, and are often very numerously attended and pecuniarily successful, being supported by the fees charged for instruction. It is not by any means true that the larger portion of the students of these Schools are graduates of Colleges; on the contrary, it is unfortunately too often the case that but little if any previous classical or mathematical training is required for admission to these special Schools. This is the fundamental difference between our system, or want of system, and that of European States. With us no government regulation requires of any practitioner of law, medicine, or theology, any particular preparation for the work he is about to enter into. There are but few municipal or State laws which place any restriction on the taking up of any profession or branch of business, no matter how much a thorough education may be really needed to make its carrying on safe to the people; all this is left to be regulated by public opinion. But in most European States, and especially in France and Germany, the case is entirely different. In those countries no student can enter any of the learned professions, take a place as Teacher in any Public School, Gymnasium, or University, or fill any post in the service of the Government, where anything more than mere menial service is required, without passing a most rigid examination, the requirements of which are strictly proportioned to the importance of the place which is to filled. It is on this foundation that the whole University system, and indeed, to a considerable extent, the whole educational system of France and Germany rests. It may be easily imagined what changes would take place in our educational institutions if every candidate for a post, either in the State or United States service, were to be required to pass before a Board of Examiners, tied down by the strictest rules, and with whom neither fear nor favor had any chance of operating.

In England, too, up to a recent period, all appointments to civil and military science, or nearly all, were made through political influence or by purchase; but gradually a great change has taken place in the system pursued in that country, and the aspirant to a public office must now prove himself possessed of some qualifications for the place, by passing an examination before a competent Board. By the introduction of this system incompetency is being gradually weeded out from all departments of the public service.

Besides the Primary Schools, Academies, Colleges, and Professional Schools, for law, medicine, and theology, there are special Schools or institutions for certain courses of instruction, of which the Agricultural Schools or Colleges, and the Polytechnic Schools, are the only ones which need be adverted to in this connection. And reference is made here only to those Agricultural and Polytechnic Schools which have an independent existence, and not to those which may be considered as existing in connection with Colleges or Universities, and which have already been noticed.

Numerous attempts have been made in the Eastern States to establish Agricultural Colleges, but they have with few exceptions proved failures. The State of Michigan was the first to put an institution of the kind in operation, and although suspended for a time, it has been started again, having received the promise of the United States grant of lands for a School of Agriculture and the Mechanic Arts. The State has made two cash appropriations for the School, one of fifty thousand dollars, ($50,000,) and one of forty thousand dollars, ($40,000,) with which lands were purchased and buildings erected at Lansing. Besides this, the College has received other pecuniary aid from the State in various ways; as for instance: a grant of a portion of the Swamp Lands, and annual appropriations for the salary and other expenses of the Secretary of the State Board of Agriculture, who is also ex officio Secretary of the Agricultural School. The Act organizing the School requiring a course of study of not less than four years, and that "the institution shall combine physical with intellectual education, and shall be a high Seminary of learning, in which the graduate of the Common School can commence, pursue, and finish a course of study, terminating in thorough theoretic and practical instruction in those sciences and arts which bear directly on Agriculture and kindred industrial pursuits." In eighteen hundred and sixty-three there were seven Professors and instructors employed in this institution.

The New York Agricultural College, located at Ovid, Seneca County, was incorporated in eighteen hundred and fifty-three. In eighteen hundred and fifty-five the Legislature passed an Act loaning this College forty thousand dollars for twenty years, without interest, on condition that an equal sum should be raised by subscription, which was done, and a farm of seven hundred acres purchased and large buildings erected. The College was opened December first, eighteen hundred and sixty, but closed after a short period, in consequence of financial difficulties, and the loss of the President, Major Patrick, who is now in the Army.

Besides the Agricultural College in Michigan, there is only one other, so far as known, which is in active operation; this is the Agricultural College of Pennsylvania, which was incorporated in eighteen hundred and fifty-five, and opened in eighteen hundred and fifty-seven, after many difficulties, and which is now in full operation, with a Faculty of five Professors and two Assistants, besides Superintendents of the Farm, Garden, Nursery, etc. The College is located in Centre County, and is partly supported by fees charged the students for board and tuition; the land and buildings, which are extensive and commodious, having been paid for by legislative appropriation and private subscriptions, amounting in all to from one hundred and fifty thousand dollars ($150,000) to two hundred thousand dollars ($200,000.)

Both the Michigan and Pennsylvania Agricultural Colleges are, to a certain extent, Manual Labor Schools; the students are required to labor from two to four hours a day on the farm, it being considered essential as a part of the student's education that he be taught the practical application in the field and laboratory of the principles he studies in the class room; while it is argued also that manual labor is essential to the preservation of health and the maintenance of habits of industry. The branches of study which are taught at the Michigan College are as follows: *During the first year*—Geometry, English literature, algebra, trigonometry and surveying, geology, history, and bookkeeping. *During the second* — Physics, meteorology, vegetable physiology, elementary and agricultural chemistry, botany and horticulture, rhetoric. *During the third*—Civil engineering, analytical chemistry, animal physiology, drawing, and rural engineering, logic, zoology, entomology, veterinary, and political economy.

The following is the course in the Agricultural College of Pennsylvania:

The First Year—The student studies arithmetic, elementary algebra, horticulture, elementary anatomy and physiology, physical geography, and elementary astronomy, English grammar and composition, elocution, history, practical agriculture, and the details of management on the College Farm.

The Second Year—Advanced algebra and geometry, general chemistry, vegetable anatomy and physiology, zoology and veterinary, geology, palæontology, practical agriculture and horticulture, logic, and rhetoric.

The Third Year—Surveying, navigation, levelling, drawing, analytical geometry, trigonometry, elementary calculus, natural philosophy, chemical analysis, veterinary surgery, entomology, agricultural botany, practical agriculture and pomology, political and social economy.

The Fourth Year—Analytical geometry, differential and integral calculus, engineering, drafting, mechanical drawing, quantitative chemical analysis, veterinary pharmacy, gardening, agricultural accounts and farm management, moral and intellectual philosophy.

The number of students in this School in eighteen hundred and sixty-two was one hundred and ten, and the expenses of board and tuition are only one hundred dollars ($100) per annum.

Besides the Agricultural Schools, as already noticed, there are special Schools for instruction in the sciences and arts, called Polytechnic Schools, or Institutes. The only one of these which has attained much celebrity is the "Rensselaer Polytechnic Institute," located at Troy, New York. This institution was founded in eighteen hundred and twenty-four, as a "School of Theoretical and Practical Science." In eighteen hundred and forty-nine it was reorganized as a "Polytechnic Institute," having for its primary object "the scientific and professional education of Chemists, Naturalists, Physicists, Architects, and Civil and Topographical Engineers; and for a secondary object, the scientific training of all others who, not contemplating a future professional career, are desirous to avail themselves of its instruction and discipline." For the accomplishment of these objects, the following courses of study have been established:

First—Course in Civil Engineering;
Second—Topographical Engineering; and
Third—In General Science.

The courses of instruction in these departments extend over a period of four years, but they all have the first year in common, during which the elements of mathematics and physics are taught, together with English composition, the French language, and drawing. In the Engineering course, during the second year, the following studies are pursued: Mathematics, including trigonometry and analytical geometry, physics continued, chemistry, geodesy, topographical and geometrical drawing, and the English and French languages. During the *third year*, the mathematical studies are carried as far as the calculus, physics continued, chemistry pursued in the laboratory, and applied to blow-pipe analysis and to mineralogy, geology studied, and geometrical and topographical drawing pursued. The studies of the last year's course are essentially practical and technical, and designed to fit the student, on leaving the institution, for entering at once in the practical application of science to the wants of everyday life—as in the location, superintendence, or construction of railroads, canals, water works, mills, bridges, and other public works, as well as the survey of rivers, lakes, and harbors, and the direction of their improvement. As it appears from the catalogue that at least nine tenths of the graduates of this institution take the degree of Civil Engineers, and of course pass through the series of studies given above, it is not necessary to notice the courses in topographical engineering and general science. The number of Professors and Teachers employed in eighteen hundred and sixty-two was nine or ten, and the entire number of students sixty. The charges for tuition are one hundred dollars ($100) per annum.

Among all the institutions and special Schools of education in the Eastern States, there is no one devoted to mining and the allied branches, nor is there in any College or special School a Professor of Mining Engineering, or the application of geology and mineralogy to mining. In fact, this branch of industry has received no aid from teaching in any of our educational institutions; and this is, perhaps, the reason why, of all departments of our natural resources, this is the one which has been most irregularly and unsatisfactorily developed. Mines have usually been foot balls for speculators, and vast amounts of money have been wasted in foolish undertakings, which a knowledge of geology, as applied to mining, might have prevented, or which never would have been undertaken had there been a class of educated men versed in these subjects in whom the public had confidence.

Of late years, however, a considerable number of our young men have been to Europe to obtain those facilities for instruction in mining and metallurgy which they could not find in the United States, there being always a considerable number of students from this country in the Mining School at Freiberg, in Saxony, while several have been educated at the Ecole des Mines, in Paris. A very large number of Germans, chiefly educated at Freiberg, are now employed all over the United States, in charge of mines and smelting works.

The fact, now so well demonstrated, that so large a portion of the western side of this continent is a metalliferous region, and must depend for its development on mining essentially, is a sufficient indication that the time cannot be far off when Mining Schools will be established somewhere in the United States; and, no doubt, Professorships in branches allied to mining will be instituted ere long in our Eastern Polytechnic and Scientific Schools.

But it hardly needs to be argued that all processes and conditions being so different on the Pacific slope and in the Great Basin from what they are in other parts of the world, it will be almost if not quite indispensable that our Metallurgists and Mining Engineers should be trained here, where they can have a practical acquaintance with the subjects they are studying.

We come now to the practical application of the facts stated above to the wants and means of the State of California, and will endeavor to show—

First—That there is no provision in the Congressional Acts granting lands to the State, and nothing in the Constitution of the State itself, which particularly defines the character of the proposed institution, and that therefore the Legislature is free to act in the matter within very wide limits.

Second—That the interests of the State require the consolidation of the proceeds of the grants of land for a University and for an Agricultural and Mechanical School, so that both these shall be parts of one institution.

Third—That it is not advisable, at least for the present, to organize a Collegiate Department in connection with the proposed institution.

Fourth—That the institution required by the State, and which will be best adapted to the wants of the people of the Pacific coast in a School of Practical Science, or a Polytechnic School, meaning thereby an institution where the elements of the Exact and Natural Sciences will be taught, and their practical application to the wants of everyday life, as to mechanics, mining, manufacturing, and agriculture.

Fifth—That the collections of the State Geological Survey should be eventually made over to the State University or Polytechnic School, or this institution, organized for the purposes of higher education, in accordance with the Constitution of the State, whatever its name may be; that the interests of the State demand that these collections should be placed in a fire-proof building, which may be called the "State Museum," where they will be accessible for the purposes of instruction, not only to the student, but to the general public; and that for that purpose a Board of Commissioners should be appointed to take the matter in hand, select a suitable location, and erect a building, from funds to be drawn from the State Treasury and other sources, as will be explained further on, and that this Board should also report to the next Legislature a plan for organizing and setting in motion a State Polytechnic School.

The term "Seminary of Learning," used by the Congressional Act, is one which may evidently be construed to mean any institution of education which is above the rank of a Common School. The definition of the word "Seminary," as given by Webster, is "a place of education; any School, Academy, College, or University, in which young persons are instructed in the several branches of learning which may qualify them for their future employment." There is evidently no restriction imposed by the term "Seminary," beyond that employed by the separate grants of lands for that purpose and for Common Schools, indicating clearly the intention on the part of Congress of endowing something superior in rank to a Common School.

The various States which have been the recipients of the land grants for a "Seminary of Learning," have invariably designated the institution organized in connection with the grant as a State University; thus we have the State Universities of Michigan, Wisconsin, Iowa, Missouri, etc.

These so called State Universities are generally organized on about the same plan; which is, to furnish instruction to all classes of students above the grade of primary scholars, or those learning reading, writing, and the elements of geography and arithmetic, up to those desiring to pass through a regular College course. Thus, the State University of Wisconsin, which has been some ten years in operation, has a preparatory department, in which boys are fitted for College or for business; a "commercial department," that is to say in plain language, a class in book-keeping; a normal department, or class for preparing male and female Teachers for the Common Schools; and a collegiate department, with a classical and a scientific course, the College proper including, in eighteen hundred and sixty-two, about one fifth of the whole number of students attending the different courses of the University. The State University of Iowa has about the same organization, but has also a Medical School attached to it nominally, in a city distant from the site of the University itself.

The State University of Michigan is far in advance of any other Western institution of learning, brought to this condition by the zeal and admirable executive ability of Doctor Tappan, the Chancellor. This University has a collegiate course proper, and two Professional Schools attached, namely, of Law, and Medicine; and not being encumbered with a Preparatory School, comes much nearer the idea of a University than any other Western institution.

The number of the Professors and instructors is twenty-seven; that of the students was, in eighteen hundred and sixty-two, four hundred; the value of the buildings, grounds, and endowment, is stated at five hundred and eighty thousand dollars ($580,000.) There is a valuable collection of casts for instruction in the Fine Arts and Architecture, and a well fixed Laboratory for practical instruction in chemistry and its application to the arts. A prominent feature of this University is the Observatory, until recently under the charge of an eminent European Astronomer, and furnished with excellent instruments, with the aid of which important discoveries have been made. It is painful to be obliged to add, that sectarian jealousies and political interference have done much to retard the progress of this institution; and that, of late, they have struck what is to be feared may prove a fatal blow to its prosperity.

In regard to the question of combining the State University, the School of Agriculture and the Mechanic Arts, and the State Museum, the following suggestions may be offered:

First—There is no legal difficulty in the way of such a course. There certainly can be no question of legal right in regard to the establishment of the State Museum in connection with the University; and that the School of Agriculture and the Mechanic Arts may also form a part of the University without violating the spirit of the Act of Congress, seems almost equally clear.

The conditions of the Act making an appropriation of land for an Agricultural and Mechanic Arts School require that some institution should be provided in which instruction in these branches should be given. The intention of the Act is, that the income of the money arising from the sale of the lands should be used for paying for instruction in the branches of knowledge related to Agriculture and the Arts; but as the Act expressly says, not excluding other studies of a liberal character, such as the classics. It is evident, then, that if, by a combination with some existing institution, or, if by a consolidation of the funds arising from this source with those obtained in some other way, both might be used to better advantage, no one could say that the action of Congress had been nullified.

The course taken in several of the Eastern States in regard to this very matter shows evidently what the feeling on this subject is there.

In Massachusetts, where there were three Colleges, each claiming a share of the Agricultural School Fund, the question was settled by the establishment of an entirely new institution, called the "Massachusetts Agricultural College," to which one tenth of the money received from the sale of the lands granted by Congress is to be paid for the purchase of a site; *provided*, seventy-five thousand dollars ($75,000) is raised by subscription for a building; and two thirds of the interest of the sum remaining is also given to this School or College for general purposes, the other third being placed at the disposal of the Massachusetts Technological Institute.

In some of the States where a State Agricultural College already exists, the grant of Congress has been given to that institution. This was the case in Pennsylvania and Michigan. In New York, however, the grant was not given to the State Agricultural College, but to the People's College. In Connecticut the whole of this grant was made over by the Legislature, with only one dissenting voice, to the Sheffield Scientific School of Yale College. In several of the other States, the scrip has been given to the State University. In Vermont, for instance, it is proposed, not only to consolidate the State Agricultural School with the State University, but also the two other Colleges—the Governor strongly urging upon the Legislature, in his last message, the importance of consolidating the existing weak institutions of higher instruction in the State into one properly endowed, by which course he thinks the State will be greatly the gainer.

We take it for granted, then, that there can be no possible legal difficulty in the way of uniting the grant of land for a School of Agriculture and the Mechanic Arts to that for a University.

Second—It remains to prove the necessity of the proposed consolidation in this State, and the first ground to be taken is that of economy. As has been fully shown, the amount of money which can ever be received from the University and Agricultural School grants is far too small, even combining both together, to build up one respectable institution. How absurd it would be, then, to fritter away what little we have by organizing two separate institutions, one of which must necessarily be to some degree a rival of the other.

To illustrate the loss which would ensue by separating the Agricultural School from the University Scientific School, we may refer to the department of instruction. Of the twelve Professorships which, as will be seen further on, we consider necessary to an institution of general science on a moderate scale, there are only three which are peculiar to an Agricultural School; all the others would be necessarily connected with any University or Scientific School which might be established. And as there is only one Professorship in that list which is peculiar to a Mining School, and one to an Engineering School, it follows that there are seven of the twelve Professorships which are common to all three of the courses of instruction, and that the services of these seven Professors would be equal to those of fourteen which would be required if two distinct institutions were to be built up.

And so with regard to collections and Library; all will admit that either an Agricultural, a Mining, or a Polytechnic School will need extensive collections in geology, mineralogy, and natural history. The sciences are so interwoven with each other, that no department can be successfully taught without help from the others. One Museum will suffice for all the wants of the State in the way of practical instruction in science; and, if there be only one, it will in time become a complete and valuable one; but, if otherwise, a very much larger amount of money will be expended, and even then, all will be imperfect. The same holds good in the matter of Library, physical and chemical apparatus, and other essentials which may be used in common by students of science applied to any department of art.

These considerations show, as it seems to us, most conclusively, that without consolidation of the Agricultural School with the University Scientific School, there will be great loss, and that the probable result will be two feeble and almost useless institutions, instead of one strong and successful one.

It may be argued that an Agricultural School without an experimental or model farm attached, is an absurdity, and that no arrangement should be entered into which will prevent such a farm from being attached to the institution. To this we would reply, that the Congressional grant is for a School of Agriculture and the *Mechanic Arts*, not for the former alone, and that since mining, which is one of the Mechanic Arts, is altogether the leading interest of the State, and the one to which science can render the greatest help, we have a right to consider the mining interests as well as the agricultural in the organization of a practical School, and that it is not by any means our duty, in organizing this institution, to make the mechanical department altogether subordinate to the agricultural, as it would be, if all the funds were to be expended on a farm in the country.

Again, it may be doubted whether the processes and methods of farming in California are of a nature to allow of their being successfully taught in a model farm. The State is too new, and her territory too large and too thinly populated, to allow, at least for a long time to come, of much compact and elegant farming. The great improvements to be made here will, as we concieve, be in the line of the application of capital to hydraulic enginery, rather than to experiments with manures and fertilisers. The farmers can be benefited by the expansion of mining enterprises and the creation of a market for their products by the development of mines and manufactories, far more than they would be by giving their children the opportunity of practicing farming on a small scale under the eye of a Professor.

Nothing that has been said above need be construed so as to prevent the formation of an Agricultural School, as a branch of the State University at some other locality at some future time, if the wants and means of the State should seem to justify such a course; but, for the present, we are satisfied that the interests of the large majority of the people require the consolidation of the School of Agriculture and the Mechanic Arts with the proposed Scientific or Polytechnic School of the University.

The question arises, whether an undergraduate course, like that of most or all of our Eastern Colleges and so called Universities, should form a part of the State University of California. There is no State University in the country where this is not the case; but we are inclined to believe that it will not be advisable, at least in its incipient stages, to organize our institution on the plan of an Eastern College; and the following reasons may be given in support of this opinion:

There are several Colleges, and Schools calling themselves Colleges, already organized and in operation in this State. These, like nearly all the Collegiate institutions at the East, have been established by different religious sects and denominations, and each is supported chiefly by those of the same belief. There is no reason to suppose that the establishment of a State College, however liberally it might be endowed, and however well managed, would put an end to the other Colleges, because the State Institution, being necessarily detached from all sects, would be looked on as a sort of infidel concern, and people of strong religious instincts would prefer to patronize institutions which were managed by those of their own way of thinking.

It is believed, therefore, that the Colleges already existing, and those which will undoubtedly be got up by other sects not yet represented by such institutions here, will suffice for giving the kind of instruction usually imparted in a College course; for it is reasonable to suppose that, in a State as new as California, and with its peculiar conditions, it will be a good many years before the number of persons demanding a College education will be large.

If this be the case, it would certainly be better that the State University should select some other portion of the great field of Science and Art not yet cultivated here, rather than that it should trespass on regions already occupied. By the plan proposed, the Colleges would be feeders to the State University, and thus one institution would aid in developing the other; for students coming from the College to the University School would stand higher and be more successful in their professional career than those who had a less amount of preparation—just as those students in the Professional Schools at Yale, or Harvard, who have been through the undergraduate course, have great advantages over those who have entered without this previous discipline.

It might be argued that the State University and Agricultural School Funds should, together with the geological collection, be made over to some existing College; but this seems to be rendered impossible by the fact that all the Colleges are of sectarian characters, and that most or all of them have sectional provisions in the laws by which they have bound themselves to be governed, so that the State could not join with them without violating the article of the Constitution which provides that no preference shall be shown to any religious sect or profession.

The following reasons have led to the recommendation of San Francisco as the point where the proposed University should be established:

First—It is the most populous city of the Pacific coast. The number of its inhabitants is probably now over one hundred thousand—a number at least five times as great as that of any other city this side of the Rocky Mountains. This concentration of population at San Francisco is still going on, and will undoubtedly continue for an indefinite period, as this city has natural advantages which no other point on the Pacific coast can show. It is and must remain the commercial and manufacturing emporium of the North Pacific coast of America, and however great the fluctuations in the prosperity of the State of California may be, the march of this city will be onward, since the whole region from Mexico to British Columbia contributes to its support.

Second—It is the most central point of the State. One third, at least, and probably as many as two fifths of the population of the State lives in the immediate vicinity of the Bay of San Francisco. By its system of river and bay steamers, it connects together Northern, Southern, and Central California; it is the point where all persons coming from abroad by sea must land, and from which radiate lines of communication in all directions towards the interior. A much larger proportion of the population of the State visit San Francisco than any other point. But:

Third—It is by far, and out of all proportion, the wealthiest city in the State. One third of the taxes which support the State Government is collected at San Francisco, and if the present rate of increase continues, as there is every reason to believe it will, this city will soon be paying one half the expenses of the State.

Fourth—The climate of San Francisco is equable, bracing, and healthy, and is better fitted for sustained study and vigorous intellectual effort than that of any other part of the State.

There can be no doubt that a State University, especially in a country as thinly inhabited as California, should be located where it will be accessible to the greatest number, and above all, that it should be situated in a wealthy community, since it cannot rely wholly on State aid for its development and support, but must call for assistance on those who have the means as well as the desire to do something to promote the cause of higher education. It is chiefly, in fact almost exclusively, from bequests and gifts of rich men that Yale and Harvard Colleges have been enabled to develope themselves into institutions of such magnitude and importance. Indeed, almost all the Eastern Colleges have arisen from humble beginnings by the gradual accumulation of voluntary donations, and we do not know of a single important educational institution that has relied solely on State or United States grants, excepting, of course, West Point, which is supported entirely by the United States as a military necessity.

The establishment of the Geological Survey was in fact the first step towards the production of a State University. Without the information to be obtained by that Survey, no thorough instruction was possible on this coast, either in geography, geology, or natural history; for the student of these branches requires to be taught in that which is about him, and with which he is brought into daily contact, as well as that which is distant and only theoretically important. The student of geology in California demands to be posted on California geology; he wishes to know what formations occur here, what fossils they contain, what ores and minerals characterize them. However valuable text books may be which are published at the East or in Europe, and which give an idea of the general principles of the science, and of their application to other regions, that is not enough; it is here that these principles are to be applied and made available; and it is only by the aid of the information collected by the Survey and the specimens arranged to illustrate the various departments of the work, that the student can have light thrown on these important studies. How could the Professors of Metallurgy teach this branch unless the processes employed here, and all over the country, from Mexico to Washoe and Reese River, had been studied out, described and compared, so that their merits and defects might become known and thoroughly understood. As the matter now stands, the whole science of metallurgy, as applied on this coast, is a perfect chaos; and years of the most elaborate and patient investigation will be required to elucidate the subject and place it in a condition to be made available for teaching.

So in regard to teaching natural history, which all will admit to be one of the most important branches of learning to be studied in a new country. Take botany, for instance, and we quote from an already published address of the State Geologist, "all that is known of our botany at the present time is in detached fragments, scattered through the reports and transactions of various learned societies, the journals of foreign horticultural associations, the official reports of Government Exploring Expeditions, and railroad Surveys, or in pamphlets published by individuals; works forming in the aggregate a very large number of volumes, nearly all of which are beyond the reach of the public generally, and many only to be found in a few large Libraries. These documents are in various languages, and many of them have never been translated into English. No attempt has been made to classify our botanical productions into one systematic whole, to arrange these descriptions into one volume, or series of volumes, or even to enumerate or catalogue our plants, and give the authorities where they may be found. The latter work has indeed been attempted, on a plan embracing the whole Pacific Coast; but although begun under the auspices of a high scientific institution, it has never been completed, and no part of it has ever appeared. Moreover it was proposed to be a mere pamphlet, at most, for the use of scientific men in making further investigations. No botanist in the world can tell how many species have already been described as occurring in California, while a great number have never been noticed at all; and of those which have been, the descriptions are often incomplete and inaccurate."

If a knowledge of botany is of any importance to mankind anywhere, either in its intellectual or economical bearings, it must be here in this new and active State. And all must allow that as yet we have neither the literature in an available form, nor the materials in our herbariums, to furnish what is required, and that they can only be obtained by systematic and continuous labor and study.

The collection of the Geological Survey will be of the greatest possible importance, not only for the general instruction of the people, but especially for the purposes of higher education in the University, and we do not hesitate to recommend that, as has been usually done in the Eastern States, these collections should be made over to the institution which is now proposed to be organized. When properly arranged in a building fitted for the purpose, they will form an ornament to the city where they are placed, and will attract strangers from every part of the Pacific Coast. Once the State Museum established in a suitable building, and gifts of specimens, some of which will be of great value, will undoubtedly flow in from all quarters.

Many valuable things have already been contributed by private individuals, but a much larger number would be if the donors could be certain that the articles given would be preserved from destruction by fire, or otherwise taken care of and placed where they could be seen by the public.

As the State has this valuable, and to the University, indispensable material on hand in a place where it is not protected from loss by fire, and not available for exhibition, we conceive that the first thing to be done towards putting the State University into operation is to erect a building for the State Museum, in which ample room shall be provided for displaying the geological and natural history collections, and in which they will be perfectly safe from fire. This building should be so constructed that the State may occupy it for the purposes of the Geological Survey as long as that work continues; and when that is terminated, it should be handed over to the University and placed under the charge of the officers of that institution. Whether the Geological Survey be continued or stopped, it is of importance that this building be erected at once. If the Survey is to be stopped, it must be evident to all that before the different persons who have been employed in getting together these collections, in all branches of natural history, leave the State, the materials they have collected should be arranged, labelled, and put in available form for the purposes of instruction and exchange; otherwise a large part of the value of the collections will be lost, since this can only be well done by those who are perfectly familiar with this vast mass of materials.

If, on the other hand, the Survey is continued, it is equally important that a safe locality should be provided where the constantly increasing mass of manuscripts, maps, specimens, as well as other valuable property belonging to the State, may be stored so as to be protected from fire, and where the laborious task of arranging the materials may be carried on *pari passu* with the Survey itself. A Laboratory is also indispensably required for the purposes of the Survey, and the expense incurred in fitting it up would be almost entirely lost to the State, unless it could, after the close of the Survey, be made available for the purposes of the University.

We propose, therefore, that a building be erected for the State Museum, which shall have ample accommodation for displaying and storing the State geological collections, and in which shall be room for a Library, a Laboratory, and the necessary offices for the Geological Survey, and also a lecture room, in which instruction may be given at such time as may hereafter be deemed advisable, so that the institution shall be sufficiently complete in itself to answer the purposes of a Scientific School, in case that from any cause, impossible now to foresee, nothing further should ever be done towards establishing the State University.

To establish an institution in California which shall be of real benefit to the people of this State, it is necessary that it should furnish some kind of information and instruction which cannot be obtained elsewhere. It should be something specially adapted to the wants of this side of the continent, and having, on that account, peculiar advantages for students here. Moreover, to compete successfully with Eastern institutions, it must be built upon a substantial basis, and make some approach to completeness in its organization. Parents finding that they can support their children at the East, or in Europe, while in the Professional School or College, at less than it will cost them here, will send them there unless there are strong inducements to keep them within the State.

It must be remembered that a superficial education in those branches which would be taught in a Polytechnic School could be of little use to the student, and certainly no credit to the State itself.

Students of the California University will have, at their entrance into practical life, to compete with students who have had the advantages furnished by old, well endowed, and skilfully managed institutions at the East and elsewhere. Young men will always be coming to California who are graduates of the Yale and Harvard Scientific Schools, of the Mining Schools of France and Germany, or of other institutions where thorough courses of instruction are given, and the student only allowed to take a degree after passing a severe examination. It is with these young men that those educated in this State will have to compete, and if our University adopts a superficial course, requires no examination for admission, gives degrees to all who ask for them, and endeavors only to make itself popular by opening its doors to all, and basing its claims to public favor solely on the number of names inscribed in its catalogue, there will be no results gained which will add to the reputation of California, and it will, moreover, be doing great harm to the young men whom it induces to act on the belief that superficiality and haste will ever answer the purpose where an education in practical science is concerned.

In view of what has been set forth in the preceding pages, we are most decidedly of the opinion that the form of an institution under which the State University and the Agricultural and Mechanic Art School should be at first organized should be that of "Polytechnic School," or "School of Science and Art."

The School should have for its object *the professional training of young men in the exact and natural sciences, and their application to arts, manufactures, mining, and agriculture.* We would recommend the course and system of the Rensselaer Polytechnic Institute as a general guide in the organization of the "California Polytechnic School," with such modifications as may be found desirable, and especially with the addition of courses of mining, metallurgy, and agriculture, to those established at that institute.

Such an institution, even on a moderate scale of completeness, should embrace the following distinct Professorships :

1.—Mathematics and Astronomy.
2.—Drawing and Design.
3.—General Physics and Meteorology.

4.—Mechanics and Engineering.
5.—Mining and Metallurgy.
6.—General and Agricultural Chemistry.
7.—Botany and Vegetable Physiology.
8.—Zoology and Animal Physiology.
9.—Geology and Mineralogy.
10.—Modern Languages.
11.—English Language and Literature.
12.—Practical Agriculture.

We do not intend to enter into a full plan of organization for the proposed Polytechnic School, but rather to leave this work for a special commission to be appointed by the present Legislature and to report to the next. This list of Professorships is given to show how considerable an amount of money will be required for commencing the institution even on the most moderate scale.

Supposing the whole amount of land granted by Congress for the University and the Agricultural and Art School to be sold at the highest price attainable, (one dollar and twenty-five cents per acre,) the whole amount at interest to be received, if the principal be invested in State seven per cent bonds, will be seventeen thousand and eighty-seven dollars ($17,087) annually, and it needs no argument to prove that in the meridian of California this sum will go but little ways towards the support of a State Polytechnic School which will be of any value to the community.

The grant of lands for the University, invested in the same manner, will yield four thousand and thirty-two dollars ($4,032) per annum, and no more.

If the Agricultural and Mechanic Art School Lands were all sold at one dollar and twenty-five cents ($1 25) per acre, the annual interest on the proceeds at seven per cent would be thirteen thousand one hundred and twenty-five dollars ($13,125); but this amount can never be realized from their sale, as the quantity of lands to be thrown on the market by the sale of soldiers' warrants and of Agricultural School Lands is so enormous that the value of United States Lands will be very much diminished. If the whole thirteen thousand one hundred and twenty-five dollars ($13,125) could be realized, it would support the three Professorships on the above list which belong particularly to the agricultural course of the School, namely, those of Botany and Vegetable Physiology, of Zoology and Animal Physiology, and of Practical Agriculture, and would do no more.

How absurd it appears, therefore, to insist on the establishment of a separate Agricultural School, when the funds likely to be realized from the grant for that purpose will not half pay the expenses of three Professors.

The whole value and success of the institution would be in a high degree dependent on the character, learning, and ability of the Professors selected, and it would be impossible to procure the services of the right kind of men in any other way than by giving them salaries which would be fully on a par, all things considered, with those given in the best Eastern Colleges, so that such as might be needed could be drawn from those Colleges. It will be useless to expect to command the services of men of first rate ability, at salaries for full Professorship, of less than from three thousand five hundred dollars ($3,500) to four thousand dollars ($4,000) be given, and the Assistant Professors should receive at least two thousand four hundred dollars ($2,400).

It will be seen, therefore, that we have very little faith in the success of an institution which should commence its career with an endowment which shall yield less than fifty thousand dollars ($50,000) per annum.

This would require a fund of five hundred thousand dollars ($500,000), invested at ten per cent per annum, or of seven hundred and twenty-five thousand dollars ($725,000), if invested at seven per cent. But although the State will not be likely to pay over seven per cent on the amount received into the State Treasury, ten or twelve per cent could be realized on all moneys subscribed by private individuals, or otherwise placed in the hands of the Board of Regents or Managers of the University, as such moneys could be invested by them without difficulty, and with perfect security, so as to realize that rate of interest. The amount mentioned above as necessary to carry on a Polytechnic School, even on a moderate scale of completeness, may seem large; but if we compare it with the available means of some of the Eastern Colleges and Universities, it will appear quite small, especially when we take into consideration the greater cost of living here, and how much higher all expenses connected with such an establishment as a College would be on the Pacific coast than they are on the Atlantic side of the continent. The regular income of Harvard University is about one hundred and fifty thousand dollars ($150,000) per annum, and it has over one and a half millions invested in productive property, besides all the grounds, buildings, libraries, collections, and museums belonging to the institution, which certainly cannot be worth less than two or three millions. But these figures are constantly increasing, as not a year elapses that large additions are not made by bequest or gift to the funds or property of the University.

The receipts of Yale College are about seventy-five thousand dollars ($75,000) per annum from invested funds and fees of tuition. The invested property, which is productive, is about half a million, and the value of the buildings, grounds, libraries, and collections, cannot be less than a million.

Finally, we believe that by the establishment of the proposed State Museum, and the carrying out of the measures proposed by this Board, that an honorable beginning will have been made towards the establishment of the State University, and that this is all which the present condition of the State finances, in view of the constitutional provisions against the increase of the public debt, will admit of. We believe that the prospective value of the institution, and the manifest advantages to the City of San Francisco from having it located at that point, will bring forth a generous response from the city to an appeal for a portion of the funds requisite to erect such a building as is needed, and that the means thus procured, combined with the accumulated interest on the Seminary Fund now in the Treasury, although credited to the School Fund, as has already been explained, will be sufficient for the purpose.

We further believe, that when the Board of Commissioners appointed for that purpose makes its report to the next Legislature, two years hence, the way will be made clear for raising the necessary funds from State, city, and individual liberality combined, to justify the putting in operation, partially at least, the proposed State Polytechnic School within four years from the date of this report, if California continues to flourish as she has hitherto done, and as we trust she will continue to do. And in concluding this report, we beg leave to offer the annexed draft of a law in which are embodied the ideas and provisions indicated in the preceding pages.

AN ACT

TO ESTABLISH THE STATE MUSEUM OF CALIFORNIA, AND TO PROVIDE FOR THE ESTABLISHMENT OF A SCHOOL OF PRACTICAL SCIENCE AS A BRANCH OF THE STATE UNIVERSITY.

The People of the State of California, represented in Senate and Assembly, do enact as follows:

SECTION 1. The Governor of the State of California, the Surveyor-General, the State Superintendent of Public Instruction, and the State Geologist, with three other persons, to be nominated on or before the first day of March next, one by the State Agricultural Society, one by the Mechanics' Institute of San Francisco, and one by the California Academy of Natural Sciences, are hereby constituted a Board of Commissioners for the purposes hereinafter provided in this Act.

SEC. 2. The Board of Commissioners constituted as aforesaid, shall proceed, as soon as may be, to select a suitable site for a building for the State Museum; *provided*, that if the City of San Francisco will donate a lot of land which, in the opinion of the Board, shall be properly and conveniently located, and of sufficient size for the buildings and grounds of a State University, or if any individual or individuals will do the same, and if, furthermore, the City of San Francisco, or any person or persons, will donate the sum of seventy-five thousand dollars for the erection of a building for the State Museum, the site of the said Museum and of the State University shall be permanently located at San Francisco; and if within one year from the passage of this Act the City of San Francisco, or individuals as aforesaid, shall not have provided a suitable lot, and the sum of fifty [seventy-five] thousand dollars as aforesaid, then the Board of Commissioners shall proceed to locate the said Museum and State University at such point as may be deemed best fitted to subserve the interests of the people and the cause of higher education, and may for that purpose invite proposals from all parts of the State for a site and for means of constructing said building.

SEC. 3. Whenever the Board of Commissioners shall certify to the State Controller that the site of the State University has been selected and approved as above, the Controller shall draw his warrant on the State Treasurer, who shall pay the same from the Fund hereinafter provided, to the Board of Commissioners designated above, for the sum of ————————.

SEC. 4. As soon as possible after the payment of the aforesaid warrant, the Board of Commissioners shall proceed to erect a suitable building for a State Museum, in which suitable rooms shall be provided for the safekeeping and proper display of the State geological collections, and also for a laboratory, library, and lecture room, and such other apartments and conveniences as may be necessary for carrying on the scientific work of the Geological Survey; and the said building and appurtenances shall be and remain in the custody and charge of the State Geologist or his Assistants, who shall occupy the same for the purposes of the Survey, and shall deposit and arrange, so far as can be done, the specimens collected by the Geological Corps, and such as have been and may be hereafter presented to the State Museum; and as soon as the arrangement of said collection shall be so far completed as to admit of its being done with safety and convenience, the said building, or such parts of it as may be properly opened to the public, shall be thus opened during five days of each week, and at least three hours of each day. And the State Geologist shall have authority to make such exchange with scientific societies and individuals as may add to the value and interest of the collection.

SEC. 5. It shall be the duty of the Controller and Treasurer, within one month from the approval of this Act, to take and set apart from the bonds now in the custody of the Treasurer, marked "School Fund," such an amount of said bonds as, at the average price at which they were redeemed, would be equal to fifty-seven thousand six hundred dollars ($57,600) in cash, and mark the same "Seminary Fund—Principal," and deposit the same in the State Treasury; and immediately thereafter they shall transfer from any money in the Treasury to the credit of the School Fund an amount which shall be equal to thirty-five per cent of such "Seminary Fund" bonds, as a separate Fund, marked "Seminary Interest Fund;" and on the first day of December, A. D., eighteen hundred and sixty-four, and annually thereafter, they shall transfer from the "School Fund" to the said "Seminary Interest Fund" an amount which shall be equal to seven per cent of the amount of bonds as above marked "Seminary Fund—Principal," which said Seminary Interest Fund is hereby appropriated and placed at the disposal of the Commissioners created by section one to carry out the provisions of this Act. All moneys in the Treasury which have been, or any money which shall hereafter be paid into the Treasury on account of sales of Seminary Lands, shall be by the Controller and Treasurer transferred to the School Fund, as interest or principal, as the same was or may be received.

SEC. 6. Whenever the State Museum Building, provided for in section four of this Act, shall be so far advanced towards completion that the State Geological Collections can be removed to the same, they shall be so removed, and from the time said removal is commenced, the interest accruing on the "Seminary Fund—Principal," bonds shall be and hereby is appropriated to the support and maintenance of said State Museum, for the purpose of paying the necessary expenses of arranging and taking care of said collections, and for all purposes connected with the custody and care of said buildings and grounds; and as long as said State Museum shall remain in the custody of the State Geologist, or until otherwise provided for by the Legislature, payments shall be made from said "Seminary Interest Fund" for the purposes aforesaid, on accounts and vouchers presented by said State Geologist to the Board of Examiners and audited by them; *provided*, however, that nothing in this Act shall be so construed as that the State Geologist shall receive any additional pay beyond that provided in the Act creating the office of State Geologist for any services he may render in connection with said Museum, or the arrangement and disposition of the collections therein.

SEC. 7. The Board of Commissioners constituted by this Act shall submit to the Legislature, on or before the second Monday of December, eighteen hundred and sixty-five, a detailed plan for the organization of a State Polytechnic School in connection with the State Musuem provided for in this Act.

www.ingramcontent.com/pod-product-compliance
Lightning Source LLC
LaVergne TN
LVHW011136110826
845150LV00008B/2371